HOLINESS
THROUGH WORK

HOLINESS
THROUGH WORK

A Dialogue with Msgr. Fernando Ocáriz
about the teachings of St. Josemaría Escrivá

Edited by

MARIA APARECIDA FERRARI

 Scepter

This is a translation of *Lavoro e Santità. Colloquio con Mons. Fernando Ocáriz sull'insegnamento di san Josemaría Escrivá*, copyright © 2018 Edusc, Rome, Italy.

English translation, copyright © 2020, Maria Aparecida Ferrari.

Translated by Helena Scott

Published by ScepterPublishers, Inc.
info@scepterpublishers.org
www.scepterpublishers.org
800-322-8773
New York

Cover image provided by Opus Dei Communications Office with permission.

Cover design by Jennifer Calabretta, isimplydesign, lcc
Text design and pagination by Rose Design

Library of Congress Control Number: 2019957363

ISBN: 9781594173738 (pbk)
ISBN: 9781594173745 (eBook)

Printed in the United States of America

CONTENTS

Introduction 1
—Luis Navarro

1. Historical and Theological Note
   on the Sanctification of Work 5
   —Javier López Díaz

2. Words and Images about the Sanctification
   of Work 39
   —Maria Aparecida Ferrari

3. Dialogue with Msgr. Fernando Ocáriz
   on the Sanctification of Work in St. Josemaría . . . 69

   Select Bibliography 93

INTRODUCTION

—◦◦◦—

The central part of this short book is a dialogue between some university lecturers and Msgr. Fernando Ocáriz, Prelate of Opus Dei, about the teachings of St. Josemaría Escrivá on the sanctification of ordinary work. The dialogue was part of an academic discussion held in Rome on October 21, 2017, at the close of an international conference entitled "The Heart of Work."

The actual text of the dialogue is preceded by a presentation by Maria Aparecida Ferrari of a short video, also entitled *The Heart of Work,* consisting of excerpts from filmed get-togethers with St. Josemaría in or around 1974, produced by Maria Villarino. At the conference, the launch of this short video served to lead into the dialogue with Msgr. Ocáriz. Additionally, in order to situate the reader in the topic, this book opens with a short "Historical and Theological

Note" by Professor Javier López Díaz, conference organizer and holder of the St. Josemaría Chair at the Pontifical University of the Holy Cross in Rome (Italy). At the end of the book is a selective bibliography on the Christian view of work and on St. Josemaría's teachings on sanctifying ordinary work.

My thanks go to all those who helped organize the conference, especially the Faculty of Theology and the Research Center for Markets, Culture & Ethics, as well as the conference speakers, whose papers have now been collected in five volumes of conference discussions. All together contributed to bring about a desire expressed by Pope Francis in his message to the conference: that "reflection on the Christian idea of professional work may help towards an understanding that any occupation is a place for maturing, human development, and personal fulfillment" (October 19, 2017).

Very especially I wish to thank our Grand Chancellor, Msgr. Fernando Ocáriz, for his words, which make us more keenly aware of the treasure contained for the Church in the teachings of St. Josemaría on the sanctification of work: a heritage of incalculable value in carrying out the mission of evangelizing the world at the beginning of the third millennium of Christianity.

REV. PROF. LUIS NAVARRO
Rector of the Pontifical University
of the Holy Cross
Rome, October 21, 2018

CHAPTER 1

Historical and Theological Note on the Sanctification of Work

—Javier López Díaz[1]

The purpose of this note is to provide the reader with some background to the dialogue with the Prelate of Opus Dei, Msgr. Ocáriz, on the sanctification of work, which forms the central part of this short book. The background on the dialogue offers some new explanations and clarifications that are of import to contemporary theology and the daily lives of Christians.

The expression "sanctification of work" was unknown until just a few decades ago, as such absent from theology for centuries. One only

---

1. Professor of Spiritual Theology at the Pontifical University of the Holy Cross, Rome.

needs to think of the first edition of the monumental *Dictionnaire de Théologie Catholique* in 1950, in 30 volumes and over 65,000 pages, which contained no entry for "*Travail*"—Work.[2] The first article on work in a major dictionary of theology only appeared in 1963. Its author, Marie-Dominique Chenu, O.P., wrote then that "it is a real novelty for the heading 'work' to be included in a dictionary of basic concepts of theology: an extraordinarily significant novelty with regard to Christian awareness and to theological reflection alike. It opens up a path within the traditional structure of Christian theology for advances in the recently-achieved view of the position of man in creation and history."[3]

2. An entry for "Work" was not included until a new edition of the *Dictionnaire* appeared in 1971. There it is acknowledged that "the absence of this article from the *D.T.C.* is symptomatic of a gap in theology" (*Dictionnaire de Théologie Catholique*, 17 (1971), 4216).

3. Marie-Dominique Chenu, *Trabajo*, in Heinrich Fries (ed.), *Conceptos fundamentales de Teologia*, IV, Madrid 1967, p. 368. (Original: *Arbeit*, in H. Fries (ed.), *Handbuch theologischer Grundbegriffe*, Munich 1963, p. 738).

What is the reason for this long gap? In general terms it can be said that in theology, ordinary work shared the same fate as the vocation and mission of the laity: forgotten or ignored.[4] To look at the question in more detail, though necessarily in summarized form, we must see what the notion of work primarily meant for Christian life and theological thought until the 20th century appearance of the expression "sanctification of work."

Two views of work, and the Christian view

Before the coming of Jesus Christ, two main views of work held sway in the Mediterranean world: that of the people of Israel, based on the

---

4. See Ernst Burkhart and Javier López Díaz, *Ordinary Life and Holiness in the Teachings of St. Josemaría*, vol. I, Scepter Publishers: New York 2017, pp. 3–76, with the references given there, as well as the recent work by Vicente Bosch, *Santificar el mundo desde dentro: curso de espiritualidad laical*, Madrid 2017, 252 pp.; and also: J. López Díaz and F.M. Requena (eds.), *Verso una spiritualità del lavoro professionale*, Edusc, Rome 2018.

Bible, and that of Graeco-Roman culture, especially in the Aristotelian tradition. The Hebrew world set a positive value on work, illuminated by the words of the first book of Scripture, Genesis, which shows creation as God's work (see Gen 2:2), and refers to the work of man as a cooperation with God, a certain prolongation of his creative work: "The Lord God took the man and put him in the garden of Eden *to till it and keep it*" (Gen 2:15). Although after original sin, work brings suffering and tiredness (see Gen 3:17–19), it does not lose its dignity in the Bible. The other Old Testament books show appreciation for different jobs and reprove idleness, though without making work into man's ultimate end.

In the Graeco-Roman view, by contrast, productive work was the task of slaves, as mere instruments of production. Free men had other things to do, not driven by necessity. And the summit of all of them was the contemplation of the truth, the occupation of philosophers.

The Incarnation of the Son of God is the great event that illuminates human work once and for all. God-made-man spent most of his life working as a craftsman in Nazareth (see Mk 6:3)! Christian thought in our time is rediscovering this powerful light, in order to shine it onto present-day life. It is a light that brings the Old Testament view of work to its fulfilment. In the Old Testament it is God who works in creating the world, while man continues with that work in some way. But in the New Testament, it is the very Son of God made man who works, prolonging the work of creating the world, which was made "through him and for him" (Col 1:16). Jesus Christ thus shows the transcendence of work in God's plans.[5] Working is something divine, which is not unworthy of the dignity of the Son of God.

---

5. He shows this not only through his example of working in Nazareth, but also in his teaching during his public life. When he says, "My Father is working still, and I am working" (Jn 5:17), he teaches that the Son of God made man continues the work of God the Father by his own work. See the remarks by Pope Benedict XVI in his renowned speech at the Collège des Bernardins, Paris, France, on September 12, 2008.

The consequence of this for Christians is magnificent. No longer are we merely continuing God's work of creation by our own work: it is the Son of God, living in each Christian (see Gal 2:20), who acts and works through those who have become God's adopted children, while respecting their freedom (see Rom 8:15; Gal 4:5). Christians, indeed, are not merely "other sons beside the Son" but "sons in the Son,"[6] sons who share in Christ's own filiation (see Rom 8:29) and the fullness of grace in Christ (see Jn 1:16). This is why we can "sanctify work," or to put it another way, why our work can become "God's work," a holy task that improves the world and enables the person who carries it out to grow in holiness, as a son or daughter of God, as Jesus Christ grew in Nazareth "in wisdom and in stature and in favor with God and man" (Lk 2:32).

Not only can we sanctify our work and sanctify ourselves in our work, but we can also

---

6. Vatican II, Pastoral Constitution *Gaudium et spes*, no. 22.

help sanctify other people through our work. The Holy Spirit, on making us God's children in Baptism, has made us into the Body of Christ, the Church, so that other people belong to each of us as the members of one same body belong to one another. St. Paul writes "if children, then heirs, heirs of God and fellow heirs with Christ" (Rom 8:17); and Psalm 2 proclaims, "You are my son, today I have begotten you. Ask of me, and I will make the nations your heritage, and the ends of the earth your possession" (Ps 2:8).

The inheritance of God's sons and daughters is the world and, above all, "the nations": other people. They are the great wealth that God has entrusted to each Christian to care for, serve and improve as a child of God should be cared for, served and improved, cooperating in their sanctification. This can be done in and through work, which is "a bond of union with others."[7]

---

7. St. Josemaría Escrivá, *Christ is Passing By*, no. 47.

Work Enriched by Redemption

All this wonderful meaning of work in God's plan of creation was enriched still more in the plan of the Redemption. The Son of God accepted work with all the consequences of sin, especially fatigue. He obeyed the will of God the Father to atone for the disobedience of sin and unite man with God (see Rom 5:19), as perfect mediator and high priest (see 1 Tim 2:5; Heb 4:14). On the Cross Jesus Christ showed his obedience by surrendering his life, through shedding his blood. In Nazareth he showed that total obedience by shedding sweat in his daily work, in union with the Sacrifice of the Cross. He obeyed by fulfilling the duty of every moment, with the same disposition with which he would afterwards give his life on Calvary. His work as a laborer was not just a preparation for the Redemption he would later carry out on Calvary; it was actually part of the work of Redemption.

"That was the way Jesus lived for thirty years, as 'the son of the carpenter' (Mt 13:55)," wrote

St. Josemaría. "And he was God; he was achieving the redemption of mankind and 'drawing all things to himself'" (Jn 12:32).[8] Similarly, we can say that Christians, made sharers of Christ's priesthood in Baptism and called to co-redeem with him (see 1 Pet 2:5,9; Col 1:24), cooperate in the work of the Redemption when they exercise their common priesthood in their work: fulfilling the Will of God the Father who calls them to work, and work well, with the love of God's children, in union with the Sacrifice of Calvary which is made sacramentally present in the Holy Mass. Christians, like Christ, can turn their ordinary work and their whole day into a prayer which is a "Mass."

A look at this concept in history

In the early centuries of Christianity there was no systematic theological reflection on Christ's

---

8. Ibid., no. 14.

work and the work of Christians, but all the elements described above are present in the New Testament, and were familiar to the early Christians. St. Paul exhorted them to work (see 2 Thess 3:6-12),[9] and he himself worked at his profession as a tentmaker (see Acts 18:3). They knew that they were God's adopted children (see Rom 8:15; Gal 4:6; Eph 1:3-23; 1 Jn 3:1–2), fellow-heirs with Christ (see Rom 8:17) and sharers in his priesthood (see 1 Pet 2:5,9; Heb 3:14), and all of this was not something separate

---

9. "Now we command you, brethren, in the name of our Lord Jesus Christ, that you keep away from any brother who is living in idleness and not in accord with the tradition that you received from us. For you yourselves know how you ought to imitate us; we were not idle when we were with you, we did not eat any one's bread without paying, but with toil and labor we worked night and day, that we might not burden any of you. It was not because we have not that right, but to give you in our conduct an example to imitate. For even when we were with you, we gave you this command: If any one will not work, let him not eat. For we hear that some of you are living in idleness, mere busybodies, not doing any work. Now such persons we command and exhort in the Lord Jesus Christ to do their work in quietness and to earn their own living" (2 Thess 3:6–12).

from their work, but something that unfolded in their daily work.

They did not abandon their job or profession when they joined the Church. On the contrary, they continued practicing the same jobs they had had before their conversion, as Tertullian wrote to his fellow citizens at the end of the second century. "So we sojourn with you in the world, abjuring neither forum, nor shambles, nor bath, nor booth, nor workshop, nor inn, nor weekly market, nor any other places of commerce. We sail with you, and fight with you, and till the ground with you; and in like manner we unite with you in your traffickings—even in the various arts, we make public property of our works for your benefit."[10] Nor did they lead lives apart from other men, but "display a wonderful and confessedly striking method of life,"[11] as another second-century document puts it. They belonged to the world without being worldly (see Jn 17:15). They tried

---

10. Tertullian, *Apologeticum*, Chapter 42, 1–3.

11. *Letter to Diognetus*, Chapter 5.

to live as citizens "worthy of the Gospel" (Phil 1:27). And each of them, through their work, tried to spread the faith among and around their colleagues, with so much drive that the pagan philosopher Celsus accused them of instrumentalizing their professions—shoe-makers, teachers, launderers and many other jobs—to sow the seed of the Gospel in private homes and throughout the whole of society.[12]

This was still the case at the end of the fourth century[13] as may be seen, for example, in the homilies of St. John Chrysostom, who exhorted the faithful to strive for holiness in their everyday lives.[14] Until then, the faithful maintained a lively awareness of the fact that they had been sanctified in Baptism, and were therefore called

---

12. See Origen, *Contra Celsum*, 3, 55.

13. See Sergio Felici (ed.), *Spiritualità del lavoro nella catechesi dei Padri del III-IV secolo*, Rome, 1986.

14. See Marcel Viller and Karl Rahner, *Ascetica e mistica nella Patristica*, Brescia, 1991 (first published 1939), p. 267 (Chapter 11: "La santità nel mondo"); and Pope Benedict XVI, General Audience, September 19, 2007.

to holiness, which was simply the unfolding of what they had received in the baptismal waters (see 1 Cor 1:2).

However, starting in the fourth century, with growing numbers of Christians forsaking the world to follow Christ as hermits and monks—although these would always be a minority in relation to the rest—the baptismal gifts shared by all began to be relegated to second place and very little attention was paid to their growth in ordinary life, work, and other activities in the world. Interest centered on the call received by some to embrace the particular state of religious life, and the act of consecration that sanctioned this life, as well as the practices of prayer and penance, and particular ways of practicing the virtues which characterized it.

From the fifth century onwards, when work was spoken of it was usually the work done by monks.[15] The Benedictine motto *Ora et labora*,

---

15. See, for example, St Augustine, *De Opere Monachorum—On the Work of Monks*.

"Pray and work," described the monk's day, divided between praying the Divine Office, study, and manual labor. Manual labor was valued as a means of supporting themselves and avoiding idleness, but there was no discussion of the value of secular work done by laypeople in civil society. Nor was there any reference to turning work into prayer; only to praying at one time and working at another, or at most, praying while doing manual work.

After the patristic period, from the eighth century on, the theology cultivated in monasteries followed along those same lines. From the twelfth century, scholastic theology developed in the cathedral schools and then the universities, but this likewise failed to discuss civil, secular work. Scholastic theologians, however, and especially St. Thomas Aquinas, made significant advances in the understanding of themes such as Christians' adoptive divine sonship and the common priesthood of the faithful, which were later to provide the basis for the topic of the sanctification of work. But explicit theological reflection on work in the ordinary Christian's life did not exist.[16] Testimonies to a positive view of ordinary work in the Middle Ages are found not in the teachings of theologians, but in the Christian sculptures that still adorn cathedral entrances and other works of art. These depictions of common jobs in some way reflect popular feelings about the dignity of work and imply some intuition of its connection with worship.[17]

At the dawn of the modern age, the ideas of the Reformers included a new esteem for work, attributable to the clear value given to it in the Bible (see Gen 2:15), which they took as the only source of divine Revelation. But both Luther and Calvin denied that the works of a Christian can do anything to merit personal

---

16. Some brief, limited considerations on the meaning of work may be found in Thomas Aquinas, *Summa Theologiae* II-II, q. 187, a. 3, c.

17. See Maria Ajroldi, "La spiritualità del lavoro nelle rappresentazioni medievali," in Maria Aparecida Ferrari (ed.), *Prospettive sul lavoro. Atti del Convegno "The Heart of Work,"* vol. I/5, Edusc, Rome 2018, pp. 79–89.

salvation, so that in this sense one cannot speak here of the "sanctification of work."[18] Luther "assigns the work of man in the world a function of its own, but one that is not directly relevant to salvation."[19] For Calvin, working hard and well is, when God rewards it with human results, a "sign" of faith that enables the person to hope that he or she is predestined; but nothing more than a sign.

The first industrial revolution, in the second half of the eighteenth century, brought about a profound transformation of productive work. In agriculture, textiles, and other fields, work moved on from primitive methods to the reasoned use of sources of energy for mechanized production. As a result, new conflicts arose between those who owned capital and the means of production on the one hand, and factory-workers and

---

18. See M. Rhonheimer, *Changing the World*, New York: Scepter, 2009, pp. 33–52.

19. Wilhelm Korff, "Arbeit, II. Kultur- u. geistesgeschichtlich," in W. Kasper and M. Buchberger (eds), *Lexikon für Theologie und Kirche*, vol. I, Freiburg-Basel-Rome-Vienna, 1993, col. 919.

farmworkers on the other. Workers often felt dispossessed and alienated, as Marx was to say, from their dignity and the fruits of their labors. In this period people's attitudes to work were profoundly shaped by social conflict.

It was in this cultural and social context that the Church's Magisterium began to discuss work, with Leo XIII's encyclical *Rerum Novarum*, published in 1891. This laid the foundations for the Social Doctrine of the Church. There was still no reflection about work as a means of sanctifying the person and fulfilling Christians' mission to do apostolic work. Instead, it focused on justice in employment relations, the rights of workers, private property and the connections between work and capital, and stood up for human beings and their freedom against the ideological extremes of socialism and liberalism. But all of these topics required a deeper understanding of work in itself, as a human activity whose purpose is to perfect creation and serve the family and society—work as an activity in which people can develop the virtues, unite themselves to

God, help others to find God, and improve the world. However, a few more decades had still to pass before any progress was made along these lines in either doctrine or practice.[20]

Twentieth century: "sanctification of work"

The expression "sanctification of work" referring to the ordinary work of lay people appears for the first time in a speech given by Pope Pius XI on January 31, 1927 to a group of young workers belonging to Catholic Action. The extant text is not the actual speech, but a summary published

---

20. A first approach in the field of the theology of the spiritual life is Adolphe Tanquerey's famous work, *The Spiritual Life: A Treatise on Ascetical and Mystical Theology*, which includes a short passage on "Sanctification of social and business relations" (nos. 607–610: Part I, Chapter V, Article II, § IV, section IV). It is not about the sanctification of work as such, so much as the relationships involved in it; but it is at least a step in the right direction. In other spiritual writers of the first quarter of the twentieth century, interest in the importance of work for Christian life goes no further than the observance of professional morality.

in *L'Osservatore Romano* on February 3, 1927. It includes the following phrases: "The secret to enjoying a continual encounter with Christ [. . .] is to sanctify one's daily work. [. . .] *Qui laborat orat*, he who works, prays, which means making work into prayer [. . .] It takes very little to sanctify oneself when one works: it is sufficient to have the good intention of directing one's work to God and remaining united to him, it is sufficient for the soul to avoid everything that offends the heart and eyes of God by offending against virtue [. . .] To preaching, to suffering, to his Passion, he dedicated a short time, only a few years, the last three years, the last days of his life. The rest of it he spent working, setting an example so that all may imitate him, doing the same as employees, workmen, do every day. The life of Jesus was like theirs. That being so, how should we not dare to say that a life of work is divine life, when that is what it is truly directed towards?"

A striking contrast exists between the doctrine contained in these words, and the Church at the time. They did not originate in an encyclical or other major document. The text was not even published in full and the Pope choose neither to emphasize these statements nor to refer to them.

This contrast perhaps arises from the fact that the "sanctification of work" held greater weight for Pope Pius XI and for Catholic Action to whom he spoke. For them the expression was not new. From 1925, within the J.O.C.—the *Jeunesse Ouvrière Chrétienne* ("Christian Working Youth") founded by Joseph Cardijn and later merged with Catholic Action—people had been speaking about "sanctifying work" by turning it into prayer.[21]

---

21. "They [young employees] should be able to sanctify themselves there [in their factory, office, etc.] and sanctify their work, their lives. They should be able to cooperate in the Christian transformation of the world of work, the professional milieu, and the re-Christianization of their fellow-workers—their brothers and sisters" (Joseph Cardijn, *Manuel de la J.O.C.*, Brussels, 1930, p. 19). This was the second Belgian edition of the *Manuel*, which was re-written after the first 1925 edition, and of which Cardijn does not figure as the author but the inspirer.

It is reasonable to suppose that Pius XI used the terms in his 1927 speech in the same sense as they had for his hearers.

In that context the expression "sanctification of work" had two characteristics that limited its reach. First, it referred to manual work alone. Intellectual work lay outside its scope. As well as implying a restriction to the material, this also affected its whole formal meaning. As manual work often permits one to pray while working, sanctifying work could be understood as "praying while working." Indeed, Gérard Philips, an expert on this topic, observed that perhaps there may have been, around that time, the exclusive concern to add a sort of religious dressing on to worldly life, just as pious souls say short aspirations or vocal prayers amidst their

---

Further on, it reads: "They should see that work can be the most expressive form of prayer, that it can be the most fruitful of sacrifices if it is united to the daily sacrifice of the Savior" (ibid., pp. 68–69). A J.O.C. chaplain wrote a few years later: "It is not alongside my duty that I must sanctify myself, but with, in and through it" (Raoul Plus, *Méditations Jocistes*, Toulouse, 1932, vol. II, p. 12).

work; whereas it is more important to sanctify the work itself.[22] This last idea is what St. Josemaría Escrivá would teach from 1928 onwards, as we shall see shortly.

The second limiting feature was that Cardijn's efforts during those years were directed to setting up the kind of structures and conditions of work that would not harm the workers' Christian identity. He aimed to set up trades-union type movements to counteract the influence of Marxism in factories. Here too, in advance, it is to be noted that the order of St. Josemaría's ideas was different: for him, the first thing was to teach Christians to sanctify their work amidst the variety of circumstances in which they worked.

It needs to be added that at the time of Pius XI's speech, there was no theological framework connecting the sanctification of ordinary work to the baptismal gifts mentioned above—adoptive divine filiation and the common priesthood

---

22. See Gérard Philips, *The Role of the Laity in the Church*, Fides Publishers, 1957.

of the faithful; but such a framework is needed in order to propose the sanctification of work to lay people in all its force. The time would come when a providential contribution in this regard was offered by a saint, as I shall now explain.

The teachings of St. Josemaría

The first writer whose teaching on the sanctification of work is endowed with all the elements derived from baptismal theology, and in whose writings this teaching occupies a central place, is St. Josemaría Escrivá de Balaguer (1902–1975), the founder of Opus Dei. One passage from his works reads as follows:

> Our Lord gave rise to Opus Dei in 1928 to remind Christians that, as we read in the book of Genesis, God created man to work. We have come to call attention once again to the example of Jesus, who spent thirty years in Nazareth, working as a carpenter. In his hands, a professional occupation, similar to that carried out

by millions of people all over the world, was turned into a divine task. It became a part of our Redemption, a way to salvation. The spirit of Opus Dei reflects the marvelous reality (forgotten for centuries by many Christians) that any honest and worthwhile work may be converted into a divine occupation. [...] Sanctity, for the vast majority of men, implies sanctifying their work, sanctifying themselves in it, and sanctifying others through it.[23]

St. Josemaría first referenced the connection between work and holiness in a note from March 1933, when he wrote, "work sanctifies."[24] Did

---

23. Josemaría Escrivá, *Conversations with Msgr. Escrivá*, no. 55. The first edition of the original work, *Conversaciones*, was published in 1968. A systematic exposition of St. Josemaría's doctrine on the sanctification of work may be found in E. Burkhart and J. López, *Vida cotidiana y santidad en la enseñanza de san Josemaría*, vol. III, 4th ed., Madrid 2015, Chapter VII, no. 2 (with the bibliography cited there).

24. Josemaría Escrivá, "Personal Notes" no. 970, dated March 28, 1933. Quoted in Pedro Rodríguez (ed.), *The Way: Critical-Historical Edition*, London-New York, Scepter, 2009, p. 362 (comment on no. 175 of *The Way*).

he write something about this subject earlier? If so, it has not survived, because he destroyed an older notebook.[25] In any case, he said several times that he had been preaching these terms since the foundation of Opus Dei. "Ever since 1928 my preaching has been that [. . .] the spirituality of Opus Dei is based on the sanctification of ordinary work."[26]

In the works of St. Josemaría published to date,[27] we find the expression in *The Way*, in the edition published in 1939: "Add a supernatural motive to your ordinary work and you will have sanctified it."[28] Msgr. Fernando Ocáriz

---

25. See Rodríguez, op. cit., p. 44; Andrés Vázquez de Prada, *The Founder of Opus Dei*, vol. I, Princeton NJ, Scepter Publishers, 2001, pp. 255–256.

26. Josemaría Escrivá, *Conversations with Msgr. Escrivá*, no. 34. See ibid., nos 26 and 55; *Christ is Passing By*, no. 20; *Friends of God*, nos. 81 and 210. At all these points he states expressly that his preaching on the Christian meaning of work goes back to 1928.

27. The St. Josemaría Escrivá Historical Institute (ISJE) is currently working on publishing critical-historical editions of his complete works.

28. *The Way*, no. 359.

gives an in-depth commentary on this point in the conversation published in this book, and also discusses other significant statements by St. Josemaría. Two other quotations bear mentioning:

> "Man ought not to limit himself to material production. Work is born of love; it is a manifestation of love and is directed toward love."[29]

> "I will never tire of repeating that we have to be contemplative souls in the midst of the world, who try to convert their work into prayer."[30]

The key to understanding these words is found in another phrase, taken from a homily by St. Josemaría: "There is something holy, something divine, hidden in the most ordinary situations, and it is up to each one of you to discover it."[31] That "something holy" should form

---

29. *Christ is Passing By*, no. 48.

30. *Furrow*, no. 497.

31. *Conversations*, no. 114.

part of the prayer of Christians who are seeking holiness in their work, because only then can work and prayer meet and combine into one. And the place of that encounter and combination is the "center" and "root"[32] of Christian life: the Eucharist. For St. Josemaría, indeed, professional work turned into prayer is a prolongation of the Holy Mass. That is how the ideal within his heart was to be fulfilled: "to set Christ at the summit and at the heart of all the activities of men"[33] so that he can draw everything to himself (see Jn 12:32).

In St. Josemaría's teaching, the sanctification of work is the "hinge" of sanctification in the world. Hence it is united to, and cannot be separated from, the gifts received in Baptism. The theological richness of his teaching lies in the connection of the sanctification of work with

---

32. *Christ is Passing By*, no. 102.

33. St. Josemaría, Letter dated March 11, 1940, nos. 12–13. See Ernst Burkhart and Javier López Díaz, *Ordinary Life and Holiness in the Teachings of St. Josemaría,* vol. I, Scepter Publishers: New York 2017, p. 346. See *The Forge*, nos. 678 and 685.

these gifts. Adoptive divine sonship, as a share in the sonship of Christ and in the divine nature (see 2 Pet 1:4), leads us to see work as the work of a child of God, "a divine occupation."[34] And the common priesthood is a sharing in Christ's priesthood that enables Christians to cooperate in his priestly mediation through the offering of their work to God. Thus they assist in the sanctification of others and in the configuring of society and the world according to God's will.

In other words, the common priesthood enables Christians to take possession of their inheritance as God's children, because "this world is ours: it is God's work and he has given it to us for our inheritance."[35] Thus the sanctification of work, as the response of Christians to the action of the Holy Spirit, is the action of God's adopted children who are called to take up their inheritance by exercising their royal priesthood.

---

34. *Conversations*, no. 55.

35. St. Josemaría, Letter dated April 30, 1946. Quoted in E. Burkhart and J. López Díaz, *Vida cotidiana y santidad*, vol. 2, p. 56.

St. Josemaría was not just a forerunner of the teachings of the Second Vatican Council on the universal call to holiness: ". . . the most characteristic element of the Council's teaching, and its final goal."[36] His teachings also provided and continue to provide light—a theological reference point or "*locus theologicus*"—for the future development of this doctrine.[37]

---

36. St. Paul VI, Motu Proprio *Sanctitas Clarior*, March 19, 1969; AAS 61 (1969) 149. On St. Josemaría as a forerunner of the Council, see the documentation, some of it unpublished, referenced in the article by Javier Echevarría, "Cinquant'anni dopo il Concilio Vaticano II: il contributo di san Josemaría," in J. López Díaz (ed.), *San Josemaría e il pensiero teologico*, Rome 2014, pp. 33–61.

37. For more on the connection in St. Josemaría's teachings between sanctification in the world and the Baptismal gifts, see J. López Díaz, "Chiamata universale alla santità nella Chiesa e Teologia Spirituale nella Costituzione *Lumen Gentium*," in *Mysterion* 7 (2014/2) pp. 199–222, which also highlights the importance of the Pastoral Constitution *Gaudium et Spes* (December 7, 1965) for an understanding of the universal call to holiness in the objective sense (all honest temporal activities can be material for sanctification). *Gaudium et Spes* Part I, Chapter 3 is fundamental to the Christian doctrine on work. A few weeks before the publication of *Gaudium et Spes*, a speech given by St. Josemaría in

This can already be seen in the encyclical *Laborem Exercens* (September 14, 1981) by St. John Paul II, which, although not quoting St. Josemaría directly, clearly echoes his teachings, especially in the last chapter, "Elements for a Spirituality of Work," on work as sharing in the activity of God the Creator (no. 25), the example of Jesus working in Nazareth (no. 26), and the meaning of human work in the light of Jesus Christ's Cross and Resurrection (see no. 27). Some years after the publication of *Laborem Exercens*, the doctrine of the sanctification of work was included in the *Catechism of the Catholic Church* (published in 1992), which says: "Work can be a means of sanctification and a way of animating earthly realities with

---

the presence of Pope St. Paul VI was published in *L'Osservatore Romano* of November 22/23, 1965. In this speech, St. Josemaría again said that his message of sanctification in the middle of the world, and the formational work he was undertaking in support of that message, "always has as its hinge the sanctification of each person's professional work," and that "sanctified and sanctifying work is an essential part of the Christian vocation."

the Spirit of Christ."[38] This doctrine is now, therefore, part of Christian catechesis. Pope Francis bears witness to this when he writes that in Nazareth the Son of God made man "sanctified human labor and endowed it with a special significance for our development."[39]

Present-day theology is invited to advance along these lines, not to draw up abstract theories, but to offer reasons that will encourage the faithful to sanctify their ordinary work and so light up the generations of the third millennium with the light of the Gospel. But it is also true that the lives of Christians who are resolved to put into practice the ideal of sanctifying their work will in turn motivate theological thinking. St. Josemaría, aware of the force for renewal contained in the message God had entrusted

---

38. *Catechism of the Catholic Church*, no. 2427. This point quotes the Pastoral Constitution *Gaudium et Spes*, no. 34. In more general terms, the point is based on the entire Chapter 3 of Part I of *Gaudium et Spes*.

39. Pope Francis, Encyclical *Laudato Si'*, May 24, 2015, no. 98.

to him to serve the Church, tried above all to put it into practice, and urged others to do the same: "Combining ordinary work with ascetical struggle and contemplation—something that might seem impossible, but is necessary in order to help reconcile the world to God—and turning that ordinary work into an instrument for personal sanctification and apostolate. Isn't that a great, noble ideal, worth giving one's life for?"[40]

This call has met a positive response. Guadalupe Ortiz (1916–1975), a chemistry lecturer, was beatified on May 18, 2019. Other faithful of Opus Dei awaiting the Church's decision includes the engineer Isidoro Zorzano (1902–1943), the student Montserrat Grases (1941–1959), and the Swiss engineer Toni Zweifel (1938–1989) The couple Tomás and Paquita Alvira died with a reputation for holiness in 1992 and 1994, after more than fifty years of

40. St. Josemaría, "Instruction," March 19, 1934, no. 33. Quoted in Burkhart and López, *Vida cotidiana y santidad en la enseñanza de san Josemaría*, vol. III, p. 643.

married life, nine children, and an exceptional example of holiness in their family and professional lives. All of them fought to embody the model of work and family life offered by Jesus, Mary, and Joseph, and they bore witness to St. Josemaría's teaching as a path to holiness opened up in the Church.

Rome, November 1, 2018

CHAPTER 2

Words and Images about the Sanctification of Work

—Maria Aparecida Ferrari [1]

Videos are made to be watched, not talked about. The purpose of the following pages is to lead into the central part of this book, which is the commentary offered by Msgr. Fernando Ocáriz, Prelate of Opus Dei and Grand Chancellor of the Pontifical University of the Holy Cross, to the video *The Heart of Work*[2] during an encounter with many lecturers

---

1. Lecturer in Special Ethics in the Faculty of Philosophy at the Pontifical University of the Holy Cross, Rome.

2. A seven-minute video produced and directed by Maria Villarino for the conference "The Heart of Work" at the Pontifical University of the Holy Cross, Rome, October 19–20, 2017: *https://www.youtube.com/watch?v=xaoI5XOQ0GE.*

and students held on October 21, 2017. Msgr. Ocáriz spoke in depth about the teachings of St. Josemaría and answered questions from participants in the dialogue.

Through the voice and images of St. Josemaría,[3] *The Heart of Work* offers an immersive exploration into the meaning of work as a basic dimension of human and Christian life; more specifically, of the message about attaining holiness in and through work.

Work is an essential foundation upon which every human being's life is based and built up. It is not surprising, then, that this short video about the sanctification of work as described by St. Josemaría Escrivá, has the power to awaken

---

3. It consists of a valuable collection of audiovisual material, filmed on different occasions during the catechesis carried out by St. Josemaría in encounters with large or small groups of people from many countries, especially in 1972, 1974 and 1975. For more on this material, see Juan José García-Noblejas, *Grabaciones audiovisuales*, in José Luis Illanes (ed.), *Diccionario de San Josemaría Escrivá de Balaguer*, 3rd ed., Instituto Histórico San Josemaría and Ediciones Monte Carmelo, Burgos 2015, pp. 575–579.

in viewers a desire to put his message into practice for themselves.

The Heart of Work shows that the people
who spoke to St. Josemaría came from very
diverse places, backgrounds and professions.[4] It
also demonstrates the universality of the Gospel's call to holiness and the centrality of work
to the human response to this call. This is how
St. Josemaría summarized the message God had
entrusted to him to pass on to others:

> Sanctity, for the vast majority of people, implies
> sanctifying their work, sanctifying themselves
> in it, and sanctifying others through it. Thus
> they can encounter God in the course of their
> daily lives.[5]

St. Josemaría's teaching was broad and deep.
It combines depth of content with simplicity

---

4. See Gianfranco Bettetini, "Lo stile comunicativo del beato
Josemaría Escrivá," in M. Fazio (ed.), *La grandezza della vita quotidiana*, vol. II, Edizioni Università della Santa Croce, Rome 2003,
pp. 137–147.

5. *Conversations with Msgr. Escrivá de Balaguer*, no. 55.

of expression and the fruitfulness of presentation for the idea of finding holiness in work and transforming society through it.

Work as a channel for love

Viewers feel invited to identify with the concerns and expectations of the people who talk about their own work situations in the video: "I produce and sell liquors," "I am a dentist and a mother," "I work and study," "I am an economist and work in a computer company," "I work for the security of a big shopping center," "I am a mother of a family, a housewife, and I work in public relations." The dialogue flows around the lives of ordinary people working in a wide range of jobs and situations.

In the mutual understanding that grows up between viewers, the questioners, and St. Josemaría's replies, it is not hard to trace the Gospel parable comparing the Kingdom of God to a "treasure hidden in a field, which a man found and covered up; then in his joy he goes and sells all that he has and buys that field" (Mt 13:44). The vocational gesture of work reflects the fact that God created man *ut operaretur* (Gen 2:15), to journey towards the fullness of his perfection by *working*.[6] This premise comes out in the empathy felt by viewers for the questions addressed to St. Josemaría, and how his answers resonate with them. The discovery of this ideal of finding holiness in ordinary work is a substantial part of the "treasure hidden in a field."

Without saying that work is the most important thing in life (which it is not), St. Josemaría understands and explains what makes work special within the set of temporal activities that make up the "treasure" that we have to discover and win with the help of God's grace. This can be grasped from his first words in the video:

On October 2nd, 1928, God wanted Opus Dei to be born. A mobilization of Christians

---

6. See Second Vatican Council, Pastoral Constitution *Gaudium et Spes*, nos. 34–35; *Catechism of the Catholic Church*, no. 2427.

who would be willing to sacrifice themselves for others, who would make all the paths of the earth divine, all of them . . . sanctifying all noble work, any honest work, any earthly occupation.[7]

When someone asks him explicitly, "Father, speak to us a bit about our ordinary work, because it can become burdensome, and at times it doesn't seem very glamorous . . .," his reply is full of the sort of realism that convinces and attracts:

I'm sure you are capable of converting the prose of each day into . . . poetry, into heroic verse. It's not true that your days are all the same! If you put love into each day, each day is different.[8]

---

7. St. Josemaría, in Santiago de Chile, July 6, 1974, AGP series A.4, t740706. "AGP" is the General Archive of the Opus Dei Prelature.

8. St. Josemaría, in Santiago de Chile, July 4, 1974, AGP, series A.4, t740704.

What's more important: manual or intellectual work? Whichever is done with more love for God.[9]

Yours should be a job well-done. Nothing shoddy—I don't know if you use the word 'shoddy' here. When you really love a woman, you don't give her as a gift something cheap. You give her something that requires a sacrifice. Well, with God our Lord, if we want to offer our work to Him, it needs to be well-done, with love, relishing our work, and in doing so, you also earn a living and improve your family's situation. But above all, to please God. Because work is also prayer, and work dignifies a person.[10]

Your work is prayer. Your work done with enthusiasm and for love,—as well as for earning money, why not?—is also penance.

9. St. Josemaría, in Buenos Aires, June 19, 1974, AGP, series A.4, t740619.

10. St. Josemaría, in Lima, July 13, 1974, AGP, series A.4, t740713.

Isn't it penitential for you some days? For me it is . . .[11]

Talk to Him! Talk to our Lord, say, "I'm tired! I can't take this anymore!" Say, "Lord, this isn't coming out right. How would you do it?"[12]

His words sum up the human and supernatural condition of *homo faber*, man the workman, of all kinds, at all times, from all backgrounds, in all jobs. Firstly, they emphasize that work is a treasure that belongs to the essence of what it is to be human; and it is something that is in itself good and noble. Secondly, they clarify that the element of fatigue is a result of original sin and needs to be transformed into an opportunity to co-redeem with Christ.

Work as such did not come into the world as a result of original sin, and it has an eminently positive meaning for human fulfillment.

---

11. St. Josemaría, in Caracas, August 30, 1974, AGP, series A.4, t740830.

12. St. Josemaría, in Madrid, October 22, 1972, AGP, series A.4, t721022.

Work is part and parcel of man's life on earth. It involves effort, weariness, exhaustion: signs of the suffering and struggle which accompany human existence and which point to the reality of sin and the need for redemption. But in itself work is not a penalty or a curse or a punishment: those who speak of it that way have not understood sacred Scripture properly. [. . .] Work bears witness to the dignity of man, to his dominion over creation. It is an opportunity to develop one's personality. It is a bond of union with others, the way to support one's family, a means of aiding in the improvement of the society in which we live and in the progress of all humanity.[13]

As well as witnessing to the dignity of man as God's creature, work restores an optimistic view of creation and love for the world, including material things, because all of it can be spiritualized, that is, perfected by man and experienced

---

13. *Christ is Passing By*, no. 47.

as an opportunity and means to sanctification and apostolate.

The Lord's will is that by our vocation we should show an optimistic view of creation, the love for the world that lies within Christianity. Joy should never be lacking from your work, or from your efforts to build up the temporal city. This despite the fact that at the same time, as disciples of Christ who have crucified the flesh with its passions and concupiscence (see Gal 5:24), you try to keep alive the sense of sin and of generous reparation, in contrast to the false optimism of the enemies of the Cross of Christ (see Phil 3:18) who measure everything in terms of progress and human power.[14]

---

14. St. Josemaría, Letter dated January 9, 1959, no. 19. Quoted in J. López Díaz, *Trabajar bien, trabajar por amor*, Edusc, Rome 2017, p. 154 (also (in Spanish) at *https://opusdei.org/es/ article/trabajar-bien-trabajar-por-amor/*).

Perfection Through Work

God blessed work as a call, a vocation, addressed to the very first human beings to share in God's work of creation (Gen 1:28). Work is a mission entrusted to man to be fulfilled out of love and with love, which makes each day new. The dignity of work, when it is based on love, perfects the person who does it. It is shown in the effort or even sacrifice involved, which takes on a positive meaning for the worker. It is shown in the conversation that the worker can maintain with God while he or she is working. The love with which someone works, in St. Josemaría's words, turns the prose of every day into heroic verse that is always new.

Love sanctifies

St. Josemaría's understanding of the centrality of work in a person's sanctification was not just a stroke of genius. It arose from the light given by the Holy Spirit because of his frequent meditation on the life of Jesus of Nazareth.

[Our Lord's] hidden years are not without significance, nor were they simply a preparation for the years which were to come after—those of his public life. Since 1928 I have understood clearly that God wants our Lord's whole life to be an example for Christians. I saw this with special reference to his hidden life, the years he spent working side by side with ordinary men. Our Lord wants many people to ratify their vocation during years of quiet, unspectacular living.[15]

In short, work, taken on by Christ, becomes a path to our redemption and sanctification. "It is a means and path of holiness. It is something to be sanctified and something which sanctifies."[16]

It is important to recall here the words of St. John Paul II referring to St. Josemaría's teaching:

For every baptized person who desires to follow Christ faithfully, the factory, the office,

---

15. *Christ is Passing By*, no. 20.

16. *Christ is Passing By*, no. 47.

the library, the laboratory, the workshop, the home, can be transformed into places for an encounter with the Lord, who chose to live in obscurity for thirty years. Who can doubt that the time Jesus spent in Nazareth was an integral part of his saving mission? The same holds true for us. Daily activities, even in their seeming dullness in the monotony of actions that seem to be repeated and always the same, can also acquire a supernatural dimension and become in a certain way transfigured.[17]

The key is to give one's work a supernatural motivation—love for God, which always includes service to others. This loving relationship with God and others does not conflict with the other legitimate purposes of work: the

17. St. John Paul II, Speech to the participants in the Congress held on the first centenary of the birth of Blessed Josemaría Escrivá de Balaguer, founder of the Opus Dei, January 12, 2002. *http://w2.vatican.va/content/john-paul-ii/en/speeches/2002/january/documents/hf_jp-ii_spe_20020112_opus-dei.html.*

satisfaction that comes from work well done; the money earned; improvement in standard of living; well-earned professional prestige, and the service done to society and culture; etc. The supernatural motivation of love for God is the "philosopher's stone" that transforms into "gold"—the glory of God—what can otherwise degenerate into forms of selfishness—vanity and ambition for prestige, seeing wealth as the supreme goal, desire for power over others, and so on.

> When men offer up all their cares and occupations to God they make the world divine. How often have I reminded you of the myth of King Midas, who turned all he touched into gold! We, despite our personal failings, can turn all we touch into the gold of supernatural merit.[18]

The motive of supernatural love shows that in order to sanctify the worker and the work,

---

18. *Friends of God*, no. 308.

it is not enough simply to do things technically well. Obviously, it is possible to aim for material perfection and efficiency while neglecting, or even being unaware of, its sanctifying dimension. However, each work is imperfect from the supernatural and human dimension. If the worker's perfection implies both dimensions, then supernatural perfection cannot be simply an extra, but it includes the human dimension, raising it up without denaturing it. If love is absent, the material progress of the world is worth very little (see 1 Cor 13:1–13).

The explanation is also fundamental in relation to people's need for finding fulfillment in the work they do. The supernatural perspective leads them to do their work with all the perfection they can, knowing that God makes use of their abilities, their potential, and their limitations. The essence of sanctified work is not, therefore, whether it is perfectly done from a human or technical viewpoint, but whether it is done for love of God and in service to others.

"Before God, no occupation is in itself great or small. Everything gains the value of the Love with which it is done."[19] And it is this which makes all honest work worthy of sanctification.

> It is well to remember that the dignity of work is based on Love. Man's great privilege is to be able to love and to transcend what is fleeting and ephemeral. He can love other creatures, pronounce an 'I' and a 'you' which are full of meaning. And he can love God, who opens heaven's gates to us, makes us members of his family and allows us also to talk to him in friendship, face to face. This is why man ought not to limit himself to material production. Work is born of love; it is a manifestation of love and is directed toward love.[20]

In *The Heart of Work* St. Josemaría expresses all these lessons in short, pithy phrases that combine

---

19. *Furrow*, no. 487.

20. *Christ is Passing By*, no. 48.

theological precision and specific examples. He explains the sanctification of work in ways that can be readily understood and applied. In addition, he is quick to perceive the deeper needs of the person addressing him, sometimes even before they have finished asking their question. At one point, for instance, someone begins, "I am a chauffeur for a company"—and immediately St. Josemaría opens his eyes to the practical and supernatural possibilities of his job.

> Make sure to do it well, conscientiously, in such a way that our Lord is happy with you. And you will take a step forward on your path to heaven. And one day you'll get there— you'll drive your car right up to paradise.[21]

In whatever activity, whatever circumstances, we need to give "to each moment—even to apparently commonplace moments—the dynamic echo of eternity."[22]

---

21. St. Josemaría, in Caracas, February 14, 1975, AGP, series A.4, t750214.

22. *The Forge*, no. 917.

> Our journey on earth [. . .] is a treasure of glory, a foretaste of heaven [. . .]. But it is not necessary for us to change our situation in life. Right in the middle of the world we can sanctify our profession or job, our home life, and social relations—in fact all those things that seem to have only a worldly significance.[23]

Against this anthropological and theological background, as Msgr. Ocáriz says in his comments, two dimensions mark the call to holiness that St. Josemaría taught and lived. One is that we are all called to be saints. The other is that ordinary everyday life is a path and opportunity to become holy. Any honest work can be made holy, and the true purpose of Christians' lives and actions is not to work but to become holy through work. We reach union with God and become more and more one with Christ through the action of the Holy Spirit (see 2 Cor 3:18).

---

23. *Friends of God*, no. 54.

At this point it is relevant to include an exchange between St. Josemaría and Dr. Eduardo Ortiz de Landázuri, whose cause of beatification has been opened. Dr. Ortiz had left the University of Granada to become Dean of the Faculty of Medicine at the University of Navarre which was being set up under St. Josemaría's inspiration. Years later, at a meeting with St. Josemaría, Dr. Ortiz said, "Father, you asked me to come to Pamplona and create a university, and it's been done—" Without thinking twice about it, St. Josemaría replied immediately, "I didn't ask you to create a university, but to become holy by creating a university."[24]

> We should be upright, strong, serving our Lord in the middle of the street, in the midst of our work, being a good friend to our friends, as well as an example for our colleagues.[25]

---

24. See *El Siervo de Dios Eduardo Ortiz de Landázuri, Hoja Informativa n° 12*: Prelature of Opus Dei, Newsletter from the Office for the Causes of the Saints, 83/XXXV (2012).

25. St. Josemaría, in Lima, July 13, 1974, AGP, series A.4, t740713.

The lay faithful in the Church are called by God to sanctify themselves in the multiple activities that make up their daily lives—work, family responsibilities, and social relations[26]—and that requires honesty and uprightness in all their doings.

This is why, in his speech to participants at St. Josemaría's canonization on the day after the ceremony, St. John Paul II stressed that "St. Josemaría was chosen by the Lord to announce the universal call to holiness and to point out that daily life and ordinary activities are a path to holiness. One could say that he was the patron saint of ordinary life. In fact, he was convinced that for those who live with a perspective of faith, everything is an opportunity to meet God,

---

26. These three aspects of human life go back to Scripture, where, in the first chapters of the book of Genesis, the mission God gives to the man and the woman on creating them includes working to perfect the world, forming a family, and building up society (see Ernst Burkhart and Javier López Díaz, *Vida cotidiana y santidad en la enseñanza de San Josemaría. Estudio de teología espiritual*, vol. II, Rialp, Madrid 2011, pp. 21–22, 38).

everything can be an incentive for prayer. Seen in this light, daily life reveals an unexpected greatness. Holiness is truly within everyone's reach."[27]

For Christians to become saints in and through their work, the ethical dimension needs to be present, since man is called to be honest and to work in accordance with human and Christian truth. The video includes a specific reference to scientific work.

> Love for the truth imbues the life and work of scientists. It allows them to hold their head high before the uncomfortable situations that can arise because having a commitment to honesty is not always favorable with public opinion.[28]

---

27. St. John Paul II, Speech to the pilgrims who had come for the Canonization of Saint Josemaría Escrivá de Balaguer (October 7, 2002) *http://w2.vatican.va/content/john-paul-ii/en/speeches/2002/october/documents/hf_ jp-ii_spe_20021007_opus-dei.html.*

28. St. Josemaría, Pamplona, May 9, 1974, AGP, series A.4, t740509.

This commitment to honesty must, in fact, be part and parcel of any job of work, as can be seen when St. Josemaría talks to journalists or people working in the field of communications.

> I have a lot of affection for journalists. I have recommended that they speak the truth. And this is very difficult because for a thousand circumstances, many times one can only say it half-way so as not to bother this person or that other one . . . But you, make sure to never lie and never defend an unjust cause.[29]

This same rectitude is seen in the advice given by St. Josemaría to a wife and mother who talks about how difficult it is to balance looking after her family and working in a firm's PR department, plus giving time to her Christian formation and life of piety.

> Well, in the midst of public relations you can have a private relationship with God our Lord.

---

29. St. Josemaría, Santiago de Chile, July 6, 1974, AGP, series A.4, t740706.

Look for Him in your heart. Draw near to our Heavenly Father. Tell Him that you love Him. Tell Him many times during the day. While you are doing public relations on earth, you're doing public relations for Heaven.[30]

St. Josemaría makes it clear that, insofar as it is the action of a human being, work becomes sanctified work when the person doing it prays—a kind of prayer that is a holy reality, a filial dialogue with God—taking occasion from the work itself. This is because, in St. Josemaría's words, "there is something holy, something divine, hidden in the most ordinary situations, and it is up to each one of you to discover it."[31]

Turning work into prayer means bringing together intense love, and the effort to fulfill one's duties and personal responsibilities, into a whole which has tangible, practical consequences.

---

30. St. Josemaría, São Paulo, July 1, 1974, AGP, series A.4, t740601.

31. St. Josemaría, "Passionately Loving the World," *Conversations with Msgr. Escrivá de Balaguer*, no. 114.

I am not speaking of imaginary ideals. [. . .]
We shall not attain our goal [of coming close
to God] if we do not strive to finish our work
well; if we do not sustain the effort we put in
when we began our work with human and
supernatural zeal; if we do not carry out our
work as well as the best do and, if possible,
even better than the best. And I think that if
you and I really want to, we will work better than the best, because we will use all the
honest human means as well as the supernatural ones which are required in order to offer
Our Lord a perfect job of work, finished like
filigree and pleasing in every way.[32]

This concrete application of the ideal is especially evident in *The Heart of Work* in the answer
St. Josemaría gives to some students who ask
him why Christians have a serious obligation to
study, and what to do so that their study brings
them closer to God.

---

32. *Friends of God*, no. 63.

My son, do you want us to be lazy? We have to live on this earth and each one supports himself with his own efforts. So students and young people need to study, OK?[33]

He is not simply talking about working with a will, but about doing one's work for love of God, in the awareness of the redeeming value of the sacrifice demanded by study or work, without letting that effort threaten one's inner order and peace of mind. "Offer your work, your study. And the day you don't feel like it, do it with more enthusiasm."[34]

There will happen to you, my son, the same thing that happens to everyone who works: that each day you will need 24 hours extra, such that you will always finish the day with many things left undone. Don't worry, keep calm. And after finishing one thing, start

33. St. Josemaría, in Madrid, October 24, 1972, AGP, series A.4, t721024.

34. St. Josemaría, in Seville, November 8, 1972, AGP, series A.4, t721108.

another one, with peace, as if you only had that one thing to do. Don't think about the rest, finish well what you are now doing.[35]

Leading others to holiness

With his message about the sanctification of work, St. Josemaría opens up horizons for everyone, since it means that every kind of work can be given its full potential for transforming people and society.

> For as long as there are people on earth, there will be men and women who work, who have a particular job or profession, whether intellectual or manual, which they will be called to sanctify, and to use to sanctify themselves and to lead others to a simple relationship with God.[36]

---

35. St. Josemaría, in Lima, July 29, 1974, AGP, series A.4, t740729.

36. Josemaría Escrivá, Letter dated March 11, 1940, no. 35, quoted in Ernst Burkhart and Javier López Díaz, *Vida cotidiana y santidad en la enseñanza de san Josemaría*, vol. III, Rialp, Madrid 2013, p. 151.

Go everywhere. In all places where an up-
right person can live, there we find air to
breathe. There we should be with our joy,
with our interior peace, hoping to bring
many souls to Christ.[37]

Work, any honest human job, is a path along
which God's children reach heaven. But they do
not go alone, because it is not possible to travel the
road to heaven without loving other people. Work
is thus an indispensable means for fulfilling the
great mission to co-redeem, to seek holiness and
do apostolic work, that is bestowed in Baptism.

St. Josemaría reminded people very clearly
that the most important apostolate for lay Christians is the apostolate they do in their work, by
setting an example in the practice of the virtues,
especially charity.

When people try to live in this way in the
middle of their daily work, their Christian
behavior becomes good example, witness,

_____

37. Buenos Aires, June 23, 1974, AGP, series A.4, t740623.

something which is a real and effective help to others. They learn to follow in the footsteps of Christ, who "began to do and to teach" (Acts 1:1), joining example to word. That is why, for these past forty years, I have been calling this apostolate an "apostolate of friendship and confidence."[38]

Being a good worker thus means not only trying to work competently, and practicing justice and honesty, but doing this with charity. Then God's children are recognized by their fruits (see Mt 7:20) in the sphere of their work as well as elsewhere.

To offer to God during the day your professional work in such a way that it pleases Him, each day you will do it better, with more rectitude, with more effort, with more feeling, thinking not only of yourself and your family, but the others, the whole of society.[39]

---

38. *Conversations with Msgr. Escrivá de Balaguer*, no. 62.

39. St. Josemaría, in Buenos Aires, June 16, 1974, AGP, series A.4, t740616.

The ideal of bringing the Christian spirit to other people and all earthly realities is left in the hands of every Christian. In the first place, because "Any honorable work can be prayer and all prayerful work is apostolate."[40] Furthermore,

> As you go about your work, doing your job in society, each of you can and should turn your occupation into a real service. Your work should be done well, mindful of others' needs, taking advantage of all advances in technology and culture. Such work fulfils a very important function and is useful to the whole of humanity, if it is motivated by generosity, not selfishness, and directed to the welfare of all, not our own advantage, if it is filled with the Christian sense of life.[41]

Christians are called to pursue holiness in the middle of the world, and their mission is to order and to throw light upon temporal affairs

---

40. *Christ is Passing By*, no. 10.

41. *Christ is Passing By*, no. 166.

in such a way that they may progress according to Christ's salvation, to the praise of the Creator and the Redeemer.[42]

> Your task as a Christian citizen is to help see Christ's love and freedom preside over all aspects of modern life: culture and the economy, work and rest, family life and social relations.[43]

---

42. See Second Vatican Council, Dogmatic Constitution *Lumen Gentium*, no. 31.

43. *Furrow*, no. 302.

CHAPTER 3

Dialogue with Msgr. Fernando Ocáriz on the Sanctification of Work in St. Josemaría

Prof. Maria Aparecida Ferrari: I would like to start by inviting Msgr. Fernando Ocáriz to offer some remarks on the short video *The Heart of Work*,[1] whose first screening we have just watched.

I think that almost all the basic elements of St. Josemaría's message on the sanctification of work are present in the video. In the first place, work is something that can be offered to God, and one of the conditions for this is that the worker tries to do it well. Secondly, all work is important, because the importance of each piece of work depends on the love with which it is done. And finally, service

---

1. Available at *www.youtube.com/watch?v=xaoI5XOQ0GE.*

to others through work is a necessary factor to sanctification through work.

All these elements of the relationship between holiness and work are part of a broader framework: the universal call to holiness, a key theme in St. Josemaría's teaching, which is a Gospel teaching. He always stressed that his message, the spirit of Opus Dei, is "as old and as new as the Gospel."[2] In his thought, his teachings, and his life, the universal call to holiness does not just refer to the subjective aspect, meaning the statement that everyone is called to be a saint. That is true, unquestionably, but there is also an objective aspect in that call, in the sense that all the circumstances of ordinary life are a means, path, instrument, opportunity and matter of sanctification. The video that has just been shown ends with St. Josemaría saying: "On the horizon, my children, heaven and earth seem to merge, but no: where they really meet is in your hearts, when you sanctify your everyday lives" (*Conversations*, no. 116).

2. See St. Josemaría Escrivá, *Conversations with Josemaría Escrivá* (New York: Scepter Publishers, 2007), no. 24, p.49.

I recall Roland Joffe's film about St. Josemaría during the Spanish Civil War (1936–39) [*There Be Dragons*, 2011], and specifically the scene where St. Josemaría receives light from God to found Opus Dei. At that point the film shows him writing the words "everyone" and "everything." *Everyone* is called to holiness and *all human realities*, any honest activity, can and should be a path to holiness, an opportunity for meeting Christ.

Work holds a very important place in the sanctification of ordinary life, not only because of the time we spend working, which is a lot, but still more because of its results for the person who does the work and for other people. Work is a central part of the universal call to holiness. This is revealed by God's plan for mankind as narrated in Genesis, right at the beginning of the Bible. There we learn that the world is characterized by its fundamental relationship with God, and that the creation of the first man and woman was oriented to the forming of the family—"Increase and multiply" (Gen 1:28)—and to working—"*ut operaretur*, to work" (Gen 2:15). Work and the family, together with the relationship with God, are, so to speak, the pillars that support God's plan for mankind.

The sanctification of work can be explained in different ways. St. Josemaría wrote in *The Way*, "Add a supernatural motive to your ordinary work and you will have sanctified it" (no. 359). This does not just mean adding on to one's work a sort of external devotional adornment. It goes to the heart of the very purpose of the work: the why and wherefore that determines the way it is done.

When St. Josemaría talks about a "supernatural motive" he is thinking of the final cause, in the philosophical sense. Aristotle, as St. Thomas quotes him in Latin, says that the final cause is "*causa causalitatis in omnibus causis*" which translates literally as the "cause of causality in all cases" (*In I Sent.*, d.45, q.1, a.3 / *In V Metaph.*, lect. 3, §782). Therefore, the "supernatural motive" determines the fact of working and the way of working: it leads you to work and to work well, to accomplish a task that is done well.

So, what is the "supernatural motive" that the sanctification of work depends on? It cannot be anything except the love of God and, as an inseparable part of that love, service to others. Sanctifying your work is just that: doing it for love of God and in order to serve other people, and that demands that you do it well, "professionally," as St. Josemaría often said. We must work well, because "God will not accept shoddy workmanship" (*Friends of God*, no. 55). We cannot offer him things done badly—without looking after the little details, without seeking perfection in the job being done.

When work is sanctified it contributes to the sanctification of the person who does it and is an instrument to help in the sanctification of others. St. Josemaría joined these three aspects in the phrase ". . . sanctifying their work, sanctifying themselves in it, and sanctifying others through it" (*Conversations*, no. 55). The three are inseparable, because in order to work for love of God and as a service to others, and to do it well, one has to bring the virtues into play. This brings about the spiritual progress of the subject, both in the human virtues raised up by God's grace, and by the theological virtues, with charity in the first place. Indeed, St. Josemaría used to say that work "is born of love; it is a manifestation of love and is directed toward love" (*Christ is Passing By*, no. 48). This is the root that enables work to be something really holy and sanctifying.

Sanctifying others with our work requires setting an example of working well, plus friendship. St. Josemaría laid a lot of stress on this aspect—friendship—of Christian apostolate, because where there is real friendship people share their own spiritual experience and their personal commitment to Christ.

Well, there's a lot that could be said about these topics, but maybe that's enough for now.

Prof. Santiago Sanz: In a study published a few years ago you stated that sanctifying work does not just mean doing something holy while working but making the work itself holy: the action of working. In that way the person doing the work becomes holy. Is it also true to say that the object of the work, the thing itself, becomes holy in some way?

What is holiness? It's a broad question, but one could say that holiness means belonging to God. We become holy in the measure in which, by our free response to grace, we belong to God. So, the more we belong to God through our free response to his grace, the holier we are. As regards things, they become holy in the measure in which they are offered to God. The things of this world already belong to God, because he created them, but through human freedom they acquire a new dimension. Because of our freedom, work itself, including its material aspect, can become holy, can belong *more* to God.

We also need to consider the Christological dimension, which is essential in Christianity. The offering of work to God is always done through Christ; it is an exercise of the common priesthood, which consists of sharing in Christ's priesthood and is always exercised in Christ. The very fact of being adoptive children of God is "being in Christ," and for that reason sanctified work is always work done "in Christ." Sometimes when he began work, St. Josemaría would say to Jesus, aloud or silently, "Let's do this together, the two of us." For us the only way to be united to God is through Christ. He is the Way, the only Mediator, and we can be mediators by bringing the world to God, including through work, in the measure in which we are "in Christ" and Christ's instruments.

Prof. Pilar Río: What is the connection between the dimension of worship in Christian life, and the sanctification of work?

I would say that the worship dimension of work consists basically of the exercise of the common priesthood. We are speaking of spiritual worship: offering work to God is an act of spiritual worship. St. Josemaría always highlighted the connection between offering up work and the celebration of the Eucharist. The Eucharistic Sacrifice is the center and root of the spiritual life, and therefore of the sanctification of work.

Another major feature of his teaching is the unity of one's life. Working and participating in the Eucharist are done at different times, but how can we unite the Eucharist to our work? The strength to sanctify our work and other daily activities comes ultimately from the Eucharist. All spiritual strength to work "with Christ and in Christ" comes from the Eucharist, which is the Sacrifice of our Redemption.

Prof. Philip Goyret: In the renewal of ecclesiology in the 20th century the Church's mission was presented as saving not just souls, but the whole person: soul, body, relationships with other people and with everything in creation. In the task of bringing creation back to the Creator, the sanctification of work has great importance. I would like to know how you see this question from the Church's point of view.

We first need to have an adequate understanding of the Church. If we follow the thought of the then—Professor of Theology Joseph Ratzinger, we can define the Church under three aspects. First, it is the "people of God," an unusual "people" in that it is present in many peoples but maintains its own unity. Secondly, it is the "Body of Christ." Thirdly, the Church is the "universal sacrament of salvation." Ratzinger said what defines the Church best is "Mystical Body of Christ" (see *Church, Ecumenism, Politics*, New York, 1988, pp. 3–20). And it's not a metaphor, because in Christ we really do form a body, with a shared life, which is the Communion of Saints.

The ecclesiological dimension of the sanctification of work lies in the Communion of Saints, because, in the measure in which we are living members of the Body of Christ, sanctified work has a positive repercussion on the whole Body of the Church. Building up our personal holiness by sanctifying our work means that we are sanctifying the whole Church. At the same time, we each receive the positive effect of everyone else's holiness. I think that this is the most radical ecclesiological dimension.

The Communion of Saints also includes the part of the Church that is in Heaven. At the end of time, however, there will be a glorification. The real goal of sanctification is the glorification not only of the spirit but also of the body. There will be "new heavens and a new earth" (2 Pet 3:13)—new, not just a continuation of this world—and our bodies will be glorified. St. Thomas says that the body will be so transformed by glory that our corporal eyes will see the Divinity in his corporal effects, principally the glorified body of Christ (see *In IV Sent.*, d.48, q.2, a.1, c).[3]

Prof. Amalia Quevedo: I'm especially happy that you referred to Aristotle, since I have dedicated a large part of my life to Aristotle. According to

---

3. The quotation from St. Thomas is: "[In glory,] *oculus carnis* (. . .) *inspiciet divinitatem in suis effectibus corporalibus, in quibus manifeste indicia divinae maiestatis apparebunt, et praecipue in carne Christi.*"

him, "'being' is said in many ways."[4] I would like to know what you think about this Aristotelian way of seeing things, open to a plurality of meanings, and also whether it may be connected with an ability to distinguish what is essential from what is accidental?

We must avoid the relativism that is so widespread in present-day culture, which aims to limit truth to what can be verified experimentally. In everything else, relativism claims that there is no such thing as truth and all you can talk about is sensations and personal opinions. Seeing it from another angle, Hegel considers that truth does not precede action but follows it. That is taken to its extreme by Marxism. What we need to do is to be quite clear that objective truth exists.

As to the distinction between essentials and accidentals, it is true that sometimes it may not be that clear, among other reasons because what is essential is manifested through what is

---

4. Aristotle, *Met.* 1003a33.

accidental. What's more, there are accidentals that are necessary, despite being accidentals. The fact is that "accidental" isn't always the same as "superfluous," something that can be done without. What is accidental is simply what exists in another being, and there are things that exist in another being, in the essence, and that cannot be separated from it.

Prof. Susan Hanssen: Professor Martin Schlag said yesterday that many people don't only work for money but because of a mission they have freely taken on, guided by their own conscience before God. From another angle, Professor Robert Gahl, in his presentation, showed the theatrical, dramatic nature of work done in the sight of God, who is our spectator. Would it be fair to say that according to St. Josemaría's teaching God watches us as a spectator while we work?

Is God a spectator? If "spectator" is understood in the external sense, I think God is much more than just a spectator. In the deepest sense he is always a protagonist, even when we don't know or don't want to know it, because we depend on him for everything—he maintains us in existence. Moreover, speaking of the sanctification of work, God's presence is not only the presence of someone outside, to whom we offer what we do. God is with us and within us. We work with Christ and in Christ. St. Paul says, "If we live, we live to the Lord, and if we die, we die to the Lord" (Rom 14:8). So that our relationship with God is never the sort of relationship we might have with someone who just watches us. But if a "spectator" is understood not just as someone who observes from the outside, but in the sense in which within the Blessed Trinity the Father sees the Son and those who are "sons in the Son" (Vatican II, Pastoral Constitution *Gaudium et Spes*, no. 22), then yes, it is legitimate to speak in those terms.

Prof. José Ignacio Murillo: St. Josemaría teaches people to be contemplatives in their work. However, contemplation has an essentially intellectual dimension. So my question is, is it possible to be contemplatives in intellectual work, which takes up the whole of one's attention?

Contemplation is not only an act of the intellect. For St. Thomas, it is a *"simplex intuitus veritatis"* (see *S. Th.* II-II, q.180, a.3, ad 1), *"ex caritate procedens"* (see *In III Sent.*, d.35, q.1, a.2, sol.1): an intuitive, not discursive, vision of the truth—a grace from God—which proceeds from love. If a piece of intellectual work is motivated by love, since love can also be present in the work of the mind, then contemplation is possible in that work.

In the short video we have just watched, St. Josemaría talks about turning work into prayer. He does not mean that we must be reciting vocal prayers while we work. Even when we aren't thinking about anything except the work we are doing, if we have offered it to God as spiritual worship and if we are with God, we can contemplate him in that work, if it is work that proceeds from charity.

Prof. Rosario Polo: What is the *quid divinum* that St. Josemaría speaks of, the "something holy, something divine hidden in the most ordinary situations" that it is up to each one to discover in order to turn work into prayer?[5]

The *quid divinum* ("What is Divine") (see *Conversations*, no. 114) has, I think, different connotations, many different aspects. From the existential, personal point of view, I would say that discovering the *quid divinum* is mainly about discovering an expression of God's love for us in everything: in people, in circumstances, in actual physical tasks, in difficulties. St. John says, in a sort of summary of the Apostles' experience of their relationship with Christ, "We know and believe the love God has for us" (I Jn 4:16). Discovering the *quid divinum* means seeing others and God's creatures whom he loves; and also seeing in difficulties the hidden love of God for us, even when we don't understand the reason for a

---

5. *Conversations with Josemaria Escriva*, no.114, p.177.

setback, because we need to believe in God's love, believe in what is not seen.

Prof. José Luis Illanes: Work is a human activity, so that sanctifying work does not mean sanctifying "this table that I am making," but sanctifying my activity of making the table, although both aspects go together. The table in itself is always the same, independent of whether I make it with love or without it. So I wonder whether the fact of working well is the same as Christianizing things.

It's true that sanctifying work and sanctifying oneself in one's work are two aspects that go together. Work is sanctified as the activity of the person who does it, and at the same time the world is brought closer to God. Sometimes the result of the work—"this table," as you put it—can be materially the same whether it is made with love for God or without it. But material things give God glory through us. In that sense, a table made with love for God is not the same as one made without it. Even though materially it may be the same, I think that in its relationship with the rest of the world and with God, it's different.

Dr. Maria Raffaella Dalla Valle: When we work with people who are different from ourselves, including people of other faiths, how can we try to bring them closer to Jesus? Is it a good idea to begin by talking about how God is both immanent and transcendent?

It depends on the person you are talking to. I think the first step must be friendship. Rather than talking on the theoretical level, it's preferable to share your own personal experience, talk about who God is for you. If there is genuine friendship, you'll get to the point where you can share ideas that will help the other person reflect too. And in every case, you need to pray, because faith is not something we can bestow by means of rational argument.

Prof. José Tomás Martín de Agar: Speaking of turning work into prayer, which is not merely adding vocal prayer to work, I remember what Benedict XVI said about prayer, when he described it as the profound orientation of the heart or the soul to God, which we can achieve in whatever we do; and he recalled in that context the "prayer of the heart" practiced especially by our brethren in the Eastern churches. I wonder whether sanctifying work might mean making our work into the prayer of the heart.

There comes to mind something St. Augustine says, with reference to the Gospel phrase about *"oportet semper orare et non deficere"* (Lk 18:1): the need to pray always and not lose heart. How is it possible to pray always? St. Augustine writes, "When we cherish uninterrupted desire along with the exercise of faith and hope and charity, we pray always" (*Ep. 130 ad Probam*, 9.18).[6] In the measure in which we do things for love of God, and persevere in doing

---

6. In Latin, the quotation from St Augustine reads: "*In ipsa ergo fide et spe et caritate continuato desiderio semper oramus.*"

them for love of God, that is already prayer. For our work to be prayer we don't have to be thinking about God while we work. Transforming it into prayer means offering it to God, doing it for love of God, and doing our best to finish it well.

Prof. Luis Manuel Calleja: I'd be grateful for some suggestions on work-related themes where St. Josemaría's teaching is particularly significant or innovative.

A very important field today is the link between ethics and work: the sanctification of work and ethics. Working well isn't simply a matter of technique, because all human work always has an ethical dimension. In today's world, unfortunately, the ethical dimension is neglected in many professional spheres.

Dr. Massimo De Angelis: I think you said previously that by sanctifying our work we also sanctify the product of our work. What I am wondering is whether that means that through our work we somehow become co-redeemers of things and of the world.

We should understand co-redeeming not as adding something to the Redemption accomplished by Christ, but as being channels for the fruits of his Redemption to reach other people. It is mainly about co-redeeming people, helping them through our work and the way we live our lives to come closer to God and to the means by which the fruits of his Redemption reach us—especially the Word of God and the Sacraments. This is the immediate, specific meaning of co-redemption: helping people to go to the sources of the fruits of the Redemption. Additionally, one can also speak of co-redeeming the material world, in an analogical sense, in so far as the material, structural things of the world can be a greater or lesser help to people in reaching God.

Prof. Fabiana Cristofari: The society in which I work is ruled by and orientated towards constant progress and growth. I would like to ask you, what should be the intellectual start-ing-point for attaining the soul of the sanctifi-cation of work, in spheres where working hard and well does not mean sanctifying one's work?

The central question is undoubtedly one's per-sonal relationship with God. Without that, with-out the conviction that there is a relationship with God that we must nurture and develop in our work, the concept of sanctifying work doesn't hold any meaning. The starting point needs to be one's own relationship with God.

Prof. Maria Aparecida Ferrari: It is time to close this session. I think we can best do so by thanking St. Josemaría in the first place. With God's grace and through the intercession of this "patron saint of ordinary life," as St. John Paul II called him,[7] it is possible for each of us also to sanctify daily life in all its aspects. I am grateful

---

7. St. John Paul II, *Address in praise of St. Josemaría Escrivá*, October 7, 2002. *http://w2.vatican.va/content/john-paul-ii/en/speeches/2002/october/documents/hf_jp-ii_spe_20021007_opus-dei.html*.

to Pope Francis for the words of encouragement he sent us, together with his blessing. And I would also like to thank especially our Grand Chancellor, Msgr. Ocáriz, who has honored and delighted us with his company in this session. Thank you, likewise, to all the people—organisers, technicians, translators—who have made this encounter possible by their discreet and effective work.

SELECT BIBLIOGRAPHY

I. Books by St. Josemaría

Christ Is Passing By, Scepter, New York, 1974.

Conversations with Monsignor Escrivá de Balaguer, Ecclesia Press, Dublin, 1972 (First printing 1968).

The Forge, Scepter, London – New York, 1987.

Friends of God, Scepter, London, 1981.

Furrow, Scepter, London – New York, 1987.

Holy Rosary, Scepter, London, 1987.

In Love with the Church, Scepter, London-New York, 1989.

The Way, Scepter Inc., Princeton, 2001 (First printing Chicago, 1954).

The Way of the Cross, Scepter, New York, 1990.

II. Some Documents from the Popes and the Holy See about St. Josemaría Escrivá

St. John Paul II

Homily at the Mass of Beatification of Josemaría Escrivá, May 17, 1992.

Audience for the pilgrims attending the Beatification of Josemaría Escrivá, May 18, 1992.

Audience for participants in the Congress on the Apostolic Letter *Novo Millennio Ineunte*, March 17, 2001.

Audience for participants in the Congress to mark the first centenary of the birth of Blessed Josemaría Escrivá, January 12, 2002.

Bull of Canonization of St. Josemaría Escrivá, October 6, 2002.

Homily at the Mass of Canonization of St. Josemaría Escrivá, October 6, 2002.

Audience for pilgrims attending the Canonization of St. Josemaría Escrivá, October 7, 2002.

Congregation for the Causes of the Saints

Decree on the heroic virtues of the Servant of God Josemaría Escrivá de Balaguer, Founder of Opus Dei.

Benedict XVI

General Audience, April 4, 2007.

Apostolic Exhortation *Verbum Domini*, September 30, 2010, no. 48.

III. STUDIES ON WORK IN THE TEACHING OF ST. JOSEMARÍA ESCRIVÁ

M. Belda, J. Escudero, J. L. Illanes and P. O'Callaghan, *Holiness and the World: Studies in the Teachings of Blessed Josemaría Escrivá*, Scepter, Princeton, 1997.

A. Byrne, *Sanctifying Ordinary Work: On the Nature and Spirit of Opus Dei*, Scepter, 1984.

J. M. De Torre, *Work, Culture, Liberation: The Social Teaching of the Church*, Manila, Vera-Reyes Inc., 1985.

S. Hahn, *Ordinary Work, Extraordinary Grace. My Spiritual Journey in Opus Dei*, Darton Longman Todd, Washington 2006.

J. L. Illanes, *Sanctification of Work*, Princeton, Scepter, 2003.

D. Le Tourneau, *What is Opus Dei?*, Dublin, Mercier Press, 1987.

J. Haaland Matlary, "Work, a Path to Holiness," in L. Clavell (ed.), *La grandezza della vita quotidiana*, vol. I: *Vocazione e missione del cristiano in mezzo al mondo*, Edusc, Rome 2002, pp. 155–170.

V. Messori, *Opus Dei: Leadership and Vision in Today's Church*, Washington, Regnery, 1997.

F. Ocáriz, *Love in Action – Loving God and Neighbor: a twofold commandment*, Scepter Publishers, 2017.

F. Ocáriz, *God as Father*, Scepter Publishers, 1998.

W. O'Connor, *Opus Dei: An Open Book*, Dublin, Mercier Press, 1991.

M. Rhonheimer, *Changing the World – The Timeliness of Opus Dei*, Scepter Publishers, 2009.

P. Rodríguez, F. Ocáriz, and J. L. Illanes, *Opus Dei in the Church: a theological reflection on the spirit and apostolate of Opus Dei*, Scepter Publishers, 1994.

J.-J. Thierry, *Opus Dei: A Close-Up*, New York, Cortland Press, 1975.

IV. Biographies of St. Josemaría

P. Berglar, *Opus Dei: Life and Work of its Founder Josemaría Escrivá*, Scepter Publishers, 1994.

E. Burkhart and J. López, *Ordinary Life and Holiness in the Teaching of St. Josemaría Escrivá*, vol. I, Scepter Publishers, 2017.

C. Cavalleri (ed.), *40 Years With a Saint: Blessed Alvaro del Portillo on St. Josemaría Escrivá*, Scepter Publishers, 1996.

J. F. Coverdale, *Uncommon Faith: The Early Years of Opus Dei (1928–1943)*, Scepter Publishers, 2002.

J. Escrivá, *The Way: Critical-Historical Edition prepared by Pedro Rodríguez*, London and New York, Scepter, 2009.

F. Faus, *A Man Who Knew How to Forgive: Incidents from the Life of St. Josemaría Escrivá*, Scepter Publishers, 2011.

M. Fazio, *Last of the Romantics: St. Josemaría in the 21st Century*, Scepter Publishers, 2018.

F. Gondrand, *At God's Pace*, Scepter Publishers, 1989.

D. M. Helming, *Footprints in the Snow: A Pictorial Biography of St. Josemaría Escrivá*, Scepter Publishers, 1986.

W. Keenan, *The Day the Bells Rang Out*, St. Albans, Batchwood Press, 2013.

W. Keenan, *The Path Through the Mountains*, St. Albans, Batchwood Press, 2015.

W. Keenan, *To the Ends of the Earth*, St. Albans, Batchwood Press, 2015.

M. M. Kennedy, *The Donkey at the Waterwheel: The Lay Spirituality of St. Josemaría Escrivá*, Scepter Publishers, 2017.

P. Urbano, *The Man of Villa Tevere*, Scepter Publishers, 2002.

A. Vázquez de Prada, *The Founder of Opus Dei*, Volume I *The Early Years*, Scepter Publishers, 2001.

A. Vázquez de Prada, *The Founder of Opus Dei*, Volume II *God and Daring*, Scepter Publishers, 2003.

A. Vázquez de Prada, *The Founder of Opus Dei*, Volume III *The Divine Ways on Earth*, Scepter Publishers, 2005.